ONE
MORE
GRAIN
OF
SAND

First published by One More Grain Of Sand, 2015
info@onemoregrainofsand.com

www.secretseeker.com

Research by Jane Sarchet, Brendan Barry, Alex Whittleton and Rob Smith
Photography by Jane Sarchet and Brendan Barry unless otherwise stated below
Book design by Ben Hoo and Rob Smith
Book series design by Ben Hoo
Edited by Katie Halpin and Alex Whittleton
Printed by Cambrian Printers, Aberystwyth, Wales

A catalogue record for this book is available from the British Library.

ISBN: 978-1-910992-06-7

Photo credits: Board and knife p.228 © Destinyweddingstudio; Bath p.232 © JeniFoto; Padstow Harbour p.236 © Ian Woolcock; Panorama of Totnes p.238 © Samot; Lyme Regis harbour p.240 © Ralf Gosch; Frome p.245 © David Michael Bellis & Blue Rock Fox Productions.

Every effort has been made to trace copyright ownership and to obtain permission for reproduction of the images in this book. If you believe you are the copyright owner, and we have not requested your permission, please contact us: info@onemoregrainofsand.com

Help us update: A great deal of effort and many calories went into the making of this book, but if you think something could be improved, or you have a secret recommendation of your own, we'd love to hear from you: info@onemoregrainofsand.com

Secret Kitchen
Southwest England

by Jane Sarchet and Rob Smith

with additional contributions by Alex Whittleton

secret
seeker

CONTENTS

INTRODUCTION

Welcome to *Secret Kitchen: Southwest England*, an insider's guide to the best places to eat, buy and source the finest produce in the West Country. Over recent years, customers have been demanding more sustainably farmed, locally sourced foods, which has led to a rise in artisan growers, producers and sellers. This movement has inspired many farmers to return to time-honoured methods and traditions. And nowhere is this trend more noticeable than in Southwest England, with its deep-rooted farming culture. You'll find plenty of outdoor-reared meat, fresh fish plucked out of the nearby sea and local, organic fruit and veg on the menus of even the smallest cafés.

This book has something for everyone, whatever your budget, tastes or dietary requirements. From elegant fine-dining restaurants, backstreet bistros and earthy street-food sellers to amazing farm shops, delis, bakeries and cookery schools, we are proud to bring you such a vibrant and varied selection of 'Secret Kitchens'. Our choices are based on outstanding produce, service and expertise, or simply because they are endearingly quirky. And while, for obvious reasons, it's impossible to find a truly secret restaurant, we have included places that many locals will not have heard of, and discovered something secret about them.

HOW TO USE THIS BOOK

We have split this book into five main sections and provided a map for each of them so you can see, at a glance, which venues are located near you. The five sections are:

Restaurants, Pubs & Cafés
Delis, Bakeries & Suppliers
Farms, Markets & Street Food
Cookery Schools
Foodie Towns

The Restaurants, Pubs & Cafés section has been split into areas (by county), due to the number of venues covered. Each of these areas has an individual map to make navigation easier.

Each venue is colour coded by county (Cornwall, Devon, Dorset, Bristol & Bath and Somerset). You will find opening times and driving directions and, in the icons and ratings, information about whether the venue caters for food intolerances, is dog friendly or has excellent service. See below.

ICONS

G.   Gluten-free option

V.   Vegan option

   Wheelchair access

   Parking

   Dog friendly

   Family venue

   WiFi network

   Outdoor seating

   Sea view

Meal and drink for one person:

£   Under £10
££   Under £20
£££   £20 and over

RATINGS

Venues are rated on service, healthy food and ambience, as shown below on a 1–5 scale.

SERVICE

HEALTHY FOOD

AMBIENCE

Restaurants, Pubs & Cafés

Cornwall
Restaurants, Pubs & Cafés

Sennen
1
St Just
2
3
Penzance
4
St Ives
Hayle
Lizard
5
Helston
Camborne
St Agnes
Perranporth
6
Truro
9
8
10
Falmouth
13
Newquay
7
Mevagissey
12
St Austell
Fowey
14 Lostwithiel
Polperro
17
Looe
18
Wadebridge
11
Bodmin
15
Liskeard
Callington
Tintagel
Camelford
16
Bude
Kilkhampton
Launceston
19
Saltash
Holsworthy
Talvista
Great
Torrington
Bideford
Braunton
Woolacombe

VENUES

The Apple Tree Café
Feed your soul

SERVICE 4

HEALTHY FOOD 4

AMBIENCE 4

Summer daily 10–5,
winter Thu–Sun 10–4

££

Trevescan, Sennen TR19 7AQ
01736 872 753
www.theappletreecafe.co.uk

Getting There
Head towards Land's End and when
you get to the hamlet of Trevescan,
look out for signs to the café.

The Secret
Tucked away down meandering
Cornish lanes and only half-a-mile
from Land's End, this is the most
westerly secret kitchen in England.

Displaying art in restaurants and cafés is not a new
idea, but The Apple Tree Café does it really well thanks
to the lovely converted barn it occupies and the quality
of the art itself. Pieces by local artists add splashes
of colour to the whitewashed interior, where winter
visitors warm themselves on sofas next to the wood-
burning stove. In the summer, visitors can enjoy the
sunshine at one of the tables in the pretty garden.

Bursting with fresh, vibrant dishes, the menu fulfils the
desires of meat-eaters, but excels when it comes to
satisfying vegetarians. Options include sprouted salads,
homemade coleslaw and even a vegetarian version of
a full 'Cornish' breakfast. The menu covers most food
intolerances, and alterations can happily be made to
dishes by asking the friendly staff.

Speciality: Apple Tree veggie burger with homemade
cider-apple chutney and salad

Heather's Coffee Shop
Coffee & cream tea

SERVICE 5

HEALTHY FOOD 3

AMBIENCE 4

Set in an Area of Outstanding Natural Beauty overlooking the sea where meandering footpaths and stone hedgerows have created a patchwork of tiny fields, this friendly tearoom is a favourite with walkers.

Heather and her team use locally sourced ingredients as much as possible, showcasing some of the best Cornish food and drink. Expect splendid breakfasts and light lunches, as well as homemade cakes and Cornish cream teas. Also on offer is what many patrons consider to be the best coffee in Cornwall.

The café occupies the old village store, right in the heart of the village of Pendeen. Its homely, bunting-clad interior has something of the 1940s about it, and the walled courtyard at the back is lovely in summer.

Specialities: cakes, cream teas, coffee

£

Summer daily 8.30–5.30, winter daily 9–5

11 Church Road, Penzance
TR19 7SF, 01736 788 069
facebook.com/
heatherscoffeeshopcornwall

Getting There
Pendeen is on the coastal road from Penzance to St Ives (B3306). You'll find Heather's on your right, at the junction with Church Road.

The Secret
Heather's appears on the Truly Cornish Café Trail – a list of the finest independent cafés in the county.

2

13

The Old Coastguard
Through the picture window

££

Daily 12.30–2.30,
3–5.30 & 6.30–9

The Parade, Mousehole, Penzance
TR19 6PR, 01736 731 222
www.oldcoastguardhotel.co.uk

Getting There
Once in Mousehole, head along
Parade Hill, where you'll find The
Old Coastguard overlooking the sea.

The Secret
*The team here lives by the maxim
'the best things in life are simple',
and it's hard to disagree when you
sit back with a belly full of great food
and watch the waves roll in.*

SERVICE 5

HEALTHY FOOD 5

AMBIENCE 5

The Old Coastguard is just 3km east of Newlyn, and – as you might expect – there is plenty of seafood on the menu. In fact, the kitchen exploits all that Cornwall has to offer, from the freshest local fish and shellfish to Cornish beef, poultry, game, cheeses and ice creams.

Breakfast is a highlight here. Try the full 'Cornish', the Newlyn smoked salmon and scrambled eggs, or the yoghurt with homemade muesli. Or stop by later in the day for the quirky 'Not Lunch, Not Supper' (3–5pm).

There's a rough-around-the-edges atmosphere at The Old Coastguard, with its sunny painted walls, comfy sofas and big oak tables. The huge picture windows and sun terrace offer spectacular coastal views – and if you look out across the waves, you may even spot Salty the Seal sunbathing on nearby St Clement's Island.

Specialities: breakfasts, 'Not Lunch, Not Supper'

Poolside Indulgence
Lounging at the lido

When you hear the word lido, you think kids, ice cream and saucy postcards – not, perhaps, a Mediterranean restaurant. But for the people of Penzance, crusty ciabattas, antipasti platters and bowls of pasta spring to mind at the merest mention of an open-air swim, thanks to the proximity of this restaurant to the historic Jubilee Pool. Built in 1935 to celebrate King George V's silver jubilee, this lido is one of the best preserved in the country.

When you arrive at the restaurant, you're met with a sign pointing to the harbour that reads: 'All our seafood comes from over there'. This statement sets the tone for the rest of the menu, which is almost entirely locally sourced. Grab a table on the terrace and enjoy the bay views. And if you visit on a Friday night in summer, you can learn the delicate art of eating a crab with style.

Speciality: Friday Crab Nights

Easter–Oct daily from 10

£

Jubilee Pool, Wharf Road, Penzance
TR18 4HH, 07779 998 590
www.poolside-indulgence.co.uk

Getting There
Heading west on the A30, take the first exit onto the B3311. Continue onto Wharf Road and Poolside Indulgence is on the right.

The Secret
The terrace at Poolside Indulgence offers one of the most spectacular views of St Michael's Mount in town.

SERVICE

HEALTHY FOOD

AMBIENCE

4

Coast Coffee Bar and Bistro
Coffee on the coast

After a bracing walk on The Lizard, the most southerly point on the British mainland, a feed at Coast is almost certainly in order. The seafood served here is about as fresh as it comes, plucked straight from the swirling Atlantic waters that surround this rugged peninsula.

The menu also includes meat from the local butcher and vegetables, salad and eggs from nearby farms. Traditional cream teas, homemade cakes and coffee are served throughout the day.

Coast occupies a former Royal National Lifeboat Institution (RNLI) garage that opens out onto a big, sunny terrace, which is ideal in warm weather. For colder, wetter days, you can warm up on a sofa by the wood-burner with a cup of steaming hot chocolate.

Specialities: fresh fish, burgers, cream teas

Daily 9.30–9

£ to ££

Lighthouse Road, The Lizard,
Helston TR12 7NJ
01326 290 400
www.coastthelizard.co.uk

Getting There
Take the A3083 into The Lizard, and Coast Coffee Bar is on your right, after the turn-off for The Square.

The Secret
Our most southerly secret kitchen offers day-long lobster-fishing trips that culminate in an evening feast featuring the day's catch.

4 SERVICE

3 HEALTHY FOOD

3 AMBIENCE

The Pavilion Boatshed
You scream ice cream

The Pavilion Boatshed is a popular restaurant just a few seconds' walk from the beach. The owner and head chef, Matt Burrell, cooked his way around the world – working in Michelin-starred establishments in Australia and making gelato in Italy – before opening up this restaurant in his hometown of Perranporth.

The mouthwatering menu is inspired by the rich fishing waters off the Cornish coast, as well as the county's farmers and local suppliers. The house speciality is a fresh seafood platter, Taste of the Sea, which is packed with masses of fish and shellfish that's simply cooked and beautifully presented.

Have a glass of champagne or a local ale by the big beachfront windows or on the street outside if it's sunny, and watch the surf crowd go by.

Specialities: Taste of the Sea, dog-friendly ice creams

£€ to £££

Wed–Sat midday–2.30 & 6–9, Sun midday–4

Getting There
8 Beach Road, Perranporth
TR6 0JL, 01872 300 784
www.thepavilionboatshed.com

Take the B3285 into Perranporth and The Pavilion Boatshed can be found opposite the large beach car park.

The Secret
This restaurant has its own brand of ice cream, Pavilion Ice, which comes in 30-plus flavours, including seasonal specials. There are also sorbets and dog-friendly ice creams.

5 — SERVICE

4 — HEALTHY FOOD

4 — AMBIENCE

Fern Pit Café
Seafood, sarnies & sun

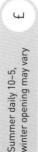

Fern Pit Café boasts extraordinary views out over the River Gannel to the open sea beyond. It lies on the Newquay side of the Pentire headland, overlooking Crantock beach, which can be accessed via a little wooden bridge from Crantock Bay at low tide.

This friendly, family-run café, which dates back to 1910, is a great place for breakfast, lunch or a snack. On the menu are traditional Cornish cream teas, homemade cakes and sandwiches generously filled with prawns and freshly caught crab.

During the summer, a ferry runs between the boathouse just below the café, Crantock beach and Newquay. At the boathouse, you can buy locally caught live lobsters and crabs or order them cooked. Feel free to ask for advice on preparing the catch at home.

Specialities: crab sandwiches, cream teas

£

Summer daily 10–5, winter opening may vary

19 Riverside Crescent, Pentire, Newquay TR7 1PJ, 01637 873 181
www.fernpit.co.uk

Getting There
From the A392, turn left at the roundabout onto Pentire Road, then onto Pentire Avenue, then Riverside Crescent; follow signs to the ferry.

The Secret
The ferry boathouse appears in three photos in The Who's 1973 album, Quadrophenia. The rowing boat in one of them, Hope, can still be seen today.

5 SERVICE

3 HEALTHY FOOD

5 AMBIENCE

7

Wildebeest
Green feast

SERVICE
⑤

HEALTHY FOOD
④

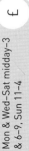
AMBIENCE
③

£

Mon & Wed–Sat midday–3 & 6–9, Sun 11–4

13 Arwenack Street, Falmouth
TR11 3JD, 01326 210 602
www.wildebeestcafe.com

Getting There
Wildebeest is on Arwenack Street, the main shopping street in Falmouth. There's parking at either end of town, and it's a pleasant walk to the café.

The Secret
From recycling and composting to biodegradable food packaging and even carbon-neutral web-hosting, this café is enviably green and clean.

If you struggle to find inspiring vegan food when eating out, then this place is likely to knock your socks off. Its mainly Japanese- and Mexican-inspired dishes use the freshest seasonal produce in such tasty combinations that even the most ardent meat-lovers are likely to feel satisfied.

Mouthwatering raw-food creations loom large on the menu, and include the likes of cucumber and shaved-asparagus salad with hoisin sauce, peanuts and a hot ginger dressing. There's also a great choice of cakes and desserts – try the warm chocolate brownie.

Tea and coffee at Wildebeest are served with a choice of dairy-free milk alternatives, including soya milk, and all wines and spirits are organic.

Specialities: vegan cheesecake, raw Pad Thai, pear and cardamom ice cream

The Secret Garden Café
Healthy hideaway

The elegant Georgian frontage of The Secret Garden Café gives way to an inviting interior that's modern, relaxed and buzzing with atmosphere. Owned by Sasha – who trained at the award-winning Ashburton Cookery School – and her partner, Ben, the café is the result of months of dreaming and planning while creating great-tasting food on a campervan stove in New Zealand.

The menu is mostly vegetarian and features tasty lunchtime dishes such as smoky-roasted beetroot and black-bean burger with salad, harissa mayo and hand-cut potato wedges. Fun labels on the menu let diners know how many of their five-a-day are in any given dish.

And, as an antidote to all that virtuous veg, don't forget to visit the Naughty Corner for some delicious, decadent treats.

Speciality: smoky-roasted beetroot and black-bean burger

15 Kenwyn Street, Truro TR1 3BU
07949 293 399
www.secretgardencafe.co.uk

Mon–Sat 10.30–4.30

£

Getting There
The Secret Garden Café is tucked away on Kenwyn Street, a gentle walk from the hustle and bustle of Truro city centre.

The Secret
The name's the giveaway! This café has a secluded garden tucked around the back decorated with mirrors, shrubs and flower-bedecked cherubs.

SERVICE

HEALTHY FOOD

AMBIENCE

The Idle Rocks
A place in the sun

4 SERVICE

5 HEALTHY FOOD

4 AMBIENCE

Daily from 8

££ to £££

Getting There
Harbourside, St Mawes
TR2 5AN, 01326 270 270
www.idlerocks.com

The Idle Rocks is on the A3078, overlooking the harbour in St Mawes.

The Secret
Desserts can be ordered in half-portions here – perfect for youngsters and anyone trying to minimise their holiday-eating guilt.

Set right on St Mawes harbour opposite the Idle Rocks themselves, this stylish boutique hotel is known for its outstanding restaurant. Offering fresh, local and seasonal ingredients, simply cooked and served in a jaw-dropping setting, this is seaside dining at its best.

In summer, tables empty out onto a south-facing terrace where elegant parasols provide shade from the sun. The atmosphere here, with the background sounds of music, chatter and boating activity in the harbour, is lively but very relaxed – especially when you have a chilled glass of wine or a cocktail in hand.

Non-residents are always welcome in the restaurant, which – although it may not be cheap – makes for an unforgettable treat.

Speciality: ceviche, globe-artichoke tart

Sunny terrace at The Idle Rocks

Strong Adolfos
Bikes & burgers

11

SERVICE
5

HEALTHY
FOOD
4

AMBIENCE
4

Mon–Fri 8.30–4.30,
Sat & Sun 9–5

£ to ££

Hawksfield A39, Wadebridge
PL27 7LR, 01208 816 949
www.strongadolfos.com

Getting There

Heading south out of town on the
A39, Strong Adolfos is on your right,
just past the turn-off for the A389.

The Secret

*According to its droves of fans, Strong
Adolfos serves the best bacon and
maple-syrup pancakes in England
– a far cry from the limp bacon butties
served up at many a roadside café.*

Fresh, friendly and retro cool, Strong Adolfos serves
classic burgers and sliders along with tasty dahl, soups,
salads and ever-changing specials. The wine list is
limited but well researched, and there are local ales
and craft beers to sample.

If you fancy an alternative to the traditional cream tea,
then Strong Adolfos brings you cracking coffee and
cakes. In fact, it takes its coffee-making very seriously
indeed – almost to the point of nerdiness. The science
is in the brewing, the art is in the delivery.

The running theme at this restaurant is 'art, surf and
motorcycles'. An exhibition space displays the work of
emerging artists, photographers and illustrators, and
there are regular motorcycle nights. Other offerings
include a classic-car club and live-music events.

Specialities: burgers, coffee, homemade cakes

Heligan Tearoom
Tea in the garden

People come from far and wide to eat in the award-winning tearoom at the Lost Gardens of Heligan. The menu revolves around a superb array of heirloom fruit and veg, from summer salads to warming winter stews.

The Sunday roasts here are renowned, and well worth splashing out on if you don't fancy cooking your own. The cakes and scones are also delicious, so if you miss the lunch slot (midday–2.30), you can fill up on an indulgent cream tea.

In winter, the wood-burning stove becomes a focal point inside, while in the summer, visitors make a beeline for the abundant outdoor seating.

There's a charge to visit the gardens, but we highly recommend that you do – they are truly magical.

Specialities: Sunday roasts, cream teas

£

Daily 9.30–4.30

Pentewan, St Austell PL26 6EN
01726 845 100
www.heligan.com

Getting There
From St Austell, take the B3273 towards Mevagissey. At the top of the huge hill you climb, turn right and follow the signs to Heligan.

The Secret
Most of the fresh produce served in the tearoom here is grown on site. Forget food miles – we're talking 150 or so food yards from soil to plate.

③
SERVICE

④
HEALTHY FOOD

④
AMBIENCE

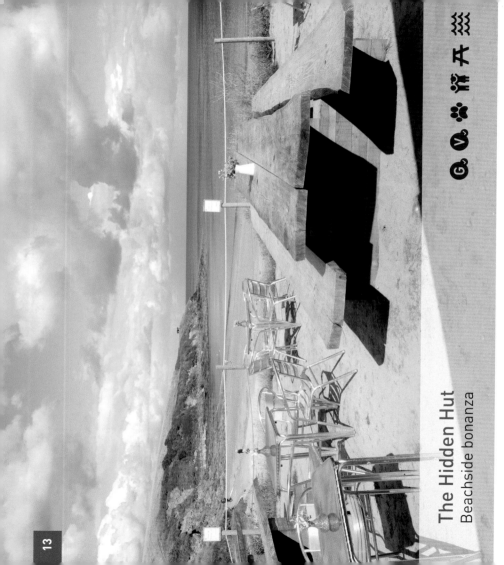

The Hidden Hut
Beachside bonanza

G Ⓥ ✿ ⛰ ⫸

£

Summer daily 10–5,
winter weekends only

Porthcurnick Beach, Portscatho,
Truro TR2 5EW

www.hiddenhut.co.uk

Getting There
Park at Porthcurnick Beach car park
in Portscatho and take a short walk
(across 2 fields) towards the beach.
Ignore the steps down to the beach and
carry on up over the brow of the hill.

The Secret
*A small café by day and a pop-up
feast venue by night, this is a beach
hut with a difference.*

5
SERVICE

4
HEALTHY
FOOD

5
AMBIENCE

They like to keep things simple at The Hut, so expect
down-to-earth, seasonal fare. Homemade Cornish
pasties, sausage rolls and cakes tend to be typical
daytime offerings, but if the weather's nice, you may
come across an impromptu barbecue or paella party.

The café also puts on regular feast nights throughout
the warmer months, when exotic recipes such as
Moroccan spiced lamb are cooked on a charcoal grill
outside. Remember to wrap up warm for these – it can
get nippy on the beach at sundown.

As its name suggests, The Hidden Hut is somewhat
tucked away, just off the coast path on the Roseland
Peninsula. The fact that you can't drive here adds to
the sense of seclusion and charm, although it makes
it hard to access for those with walking difficulties.

Specialities: Cornish pasties, feast nights

13

The Kings Arms
Like pubs used to be

If you're bored of swanky gastro pubs and in need of some honest, home-cooked food, you can't go wrong with The Kings Arms, which serves a great choice of classic pub grub and a fine selection of local ales.

All the trappings of a typical locals' pub can be found here, from the pool table, dartboard and skittle alley to the heavily patterned carpets. But it's an excellent pitstop for hungry walkers, cyclists and families, with a daily-changing specials board and popular 'build your own burger' option.

Above all, The Kings Arms is a fun place to be. On the first Wednesday of the month, it hosts a Cornish music and dance night, and during Mevagissey's midsummer Feast Week festival, live bands and the infamous Ball Race take place here.

Speciality: butternut-squash Wellington

££

Mon-Thu 11-11,
Fri-Sun 11-midnight

Bridges, Luxulyan PL30 5EF
01726 850 202
www.staustellbrewery.co.uk/pub/
luxulyan/kings-arms

Getting There
From the A30, take the A391 towards St Austell. Follow the signs towards Luxulyan, and The Kings Arms can be found just over the railway bridge.

The Secret
It's possible to walk to this pub from the UNESCO-listed Luxulyan Valley and the world-famous Eden Project.

SERVICE
5

HEALTHY FOOD
3

AMBIENCE
3

14

Woods Café
A woodland welcome

SERVICE 3

HEALTHY FOOD 3

AMBIENCE 5

£

Daily 10.30–4.30, with extended summer hours

Cardinham Woods, Bodmin
PL30 4AL, 01208 781 11
www.woodscafecornwall.co.uk

Getting There
Cardinham Woods are to the east of Bodmin. Once in the woods, head to the main car park and the café is close by and well signposted.

The Secret
You wouldn't know it, but there's a newly refurbished, two-bedroom apartment to rent above this little café. See website for details.

The pretty, stonework Woods Café in the centre of Cardinham Woods is ready to tend to the needs of weary walkers with cakes, freshly baked scones and a tempting lunch menu. Some regulars make the trip here for the delicious pulled-pork ciabatta alone.

In the café's large woodland garden, which is lovely in summer, there are plenty of tables and water bowls for thirsty dogs. In winter, weather-beaten walkers make straight for the seats nearest the roaring log fire, savouring hot chocolates and warming bowls of soup.

The surrounding woods are perfect for those with boisterous dogs or kids to wear out – or for anyone who has eaten one too many pasties on holiday and needs to stretch their legs. You'll find a playground and several walking and cycling trails here.

Specialities: cheese scones, pulled-pork baguette

Masons Arms
Rabbit! Rabbit! Rabbit!

Daily midday–2.30 & 6-9

££

Market Place, Camelford PL32 9PB
01840 213 309
www.masonsarmscamelford.co.uk

Getting There

The Masons Arms is easily located on Market Place (A39) in Camelford. Conveniently, there is a public car park just a short walk away.

The Secret

If you're celebrating a special occasion, call ahead and the landlady, Jo, and her team will decorate the table and organise a cake for you.

SERVICE
3

HEALTHY FOOD
3

AMBIENCE
3

When visiting the Masons Arms, we recommend ignoring the regular menu in favour of the impressive specials board. Typical dishes include lamb's liver with bacon and onion gravy and a Rabbit Duo – rabbit pie and pan-fried rabbit loin in a wine sauce with Dauphinoise potatoes and seasonal veg. A separate fish menu celebrates locally landed seafood, and there are plenty of options for vegetarians.

Run by the same team for 20 years, the pub is known for its ever-expanding collection of interesting artefacts and quirky memorabilia that – quite literally – covers the interior (including the ceiling). The result is rather chaotic, but also very charming.

In good weather, the beer garden, which backs onto the River Camel, fills up fast. Dogs on leads are welcome.

Specialities: home-reared lamb, seafood, game

Talland Bay Beach Café
Beside the seaside

This café has huge appeal, thanks to its beautiful beachside location, outstanding views, lovely food and quirky seating areas. Opt for a stool by the big windows overlooking the beach, a bench beneath a bright-blue parasol or one of the beautifully decorated beach huts that are kitted out with shabby-chic tables and chairs.

When it comes to food at Talland Bay Beach Café, expect light bites: paninis, pasties and soup, cakes, cream teas and Cornish ice creams. The coffee is freshly ground and really good.

The small pebbly beach in front of the café is very sheltered and great for kids. It's the perfect place for swimming, exploring rock pools and kayaking. At low tide, a giant sandbank appears, which provides no end of paddling and sandcastle fun.

Specialities: ice creams, coffee, homemade cakes

SERVICE 3

HEALTHY FOOD 3

AMBIENCE 4

£

Mid-Mar–end Oct
daily 9–5.30

Talland, Looe PL13 2JA
01503 272 088
www.tallandbaybeachcafe.co.uk

Getting There
On the Looe-to-Polperro road (A387), simply follow the signs to Talland Bay. The lanes are very narrow in places, so drive with extra caution.

The Secret
This café has an on-site beach shop that offers a kayak-hire service; the kayaks are single-seaters, but can hold an adult with a small child.

Ocean & Earth
Heaven on a plate

Anyone who has visited Thailand and misses its fragrant cuisine should eat at Ocean & Earth. This intimate and beautifully decorated restaurant blends the very best local ingredients with signature Asian flavours, creating mouthwatering Thai fare with a lovely Cornish twist.

You'll find old favourites on the menu, such as Pad Thai noodles with a zingy papaya salad and Thai green curry with coconut milk and fresh spices. The chefs are very imaginative with their specials, bringing diners some refreshingly unusual combinations.

Occasionally, the restaurant hosts special events to celebrate festivals in the Thai calendar. These evenings tend to be very popular, so it's advisable to book ahead. If you're too late, however, there's always the excellent takeaway service.

Specialities: Thai green curry, Tom Yam Gai

££

Summer Mon–Sat 5–11,
Sun 6–10.30

Higher Market Street, East Looe
PL13 1BF, 01503 263 080
www.oceanandearththairestaurant.co.uk

Getting There
Wander through the streets of Looe down towards the beach, taking the left turn at Mountain Warehouse onto Higher Market Street.

The Secret
This exceptional restaurant offers a catering service for functions and dinner parties, in your own home or elsewhere.

5 — SERVICE

5 — HEALTHY FOOD

4 — AMBIENCE

The Springer Spaniel
All in the game

SERVICE 4

HEALTHY FOOD 3

AMBIENCE 4

Mon–Sat midday–3 & 6–9 | ££

Treburley, Launceston PL15 9NS
01579 370 424
www.thespringerspaniel.co.uk

Getting There
The Springer Spaniel is situated on the A388 between Callington and Launceston.

The Secret
The owner of The Springer Spaniel is none other than the Masterchef 2012 winner, Anton Piotrowski, who has big plans for this 18th-century pub.

The Springer Spaniel is a traditional country pub with a welcoming, lively atmosphere and crackling open fires. And with several menus to choose from, it's a top choice for families and big groups.

For a slap-up lunch, try the upmarket yet classic bar menu, with its steak sandwich with fried egg and triple-cooked chips – artery-clogging but utterly delicious. There's also a menu for kids (otherwise known as 'Springer pups') and a spectacular fine-dining taster menu, which features seven courses.

There's an emphasis on game at this pub, as its hunting-inspired décor suggests, with duck, venison, guinea fowl and pheasant dishes making regular appearances on the menu. And though the food is classy, the atmosphere remains unpretentious.

Specialities: game, desserts

Devon
Restaurants, Pubs & Cafés

Penarth
Weston-super-
Berrow
Burnham-on-
Llantwit Major
Barry
Bridgwater
Weston-super-
Minehead
Watchet
Taunton
Wiveliscombe
Wellington
Ilminster
Chard
Axminster
Seaton
Sidbury
Sidmouth
Honiton
Dulverton
Bampton
Tiverton 39 Willand
Cullompton
Broadclyst
Topsham 38 Exmouth
Exeter
36
Crediton
Chulmleigh Witheridge
Lynton
32
30
25
Swimbridge
South Molton
Barnstaple
Braunton
Bideford
22
20
Great Torrington
23
Hatherleigh
26
Holsworthy
Okehampton
Moretonhampstead 37 Chudleigh
33
29
35
Newton Abbot
Kingkerswell
Torquay
Paignton
Brixham
Dartmouth
Kingsbridge 34
Salcombe 31
Kilkhampton
Bude
Launceston
Callington
Tavistock
Yelverton
Woolwell
Wembury
Plymouth 21
Saltash
Ivybridge 27
Modbury
28
South Brent
Liskeard
Looe
Polperro
Woolacombe
Ilfracombe

42

The Pig on the Hill
Piggy pub grub

SERVICE 5

HEALTHY FOOD 4

AMBIENCE 5

The Pig on The Hill occupies a converted cowshed set in beautiful countryside only a short distance from the sea. With its down-to-earth atmosphere and good-quality food, the pub has a loyal band of regulars from across the local area.

The chefs stop at nothing in search of outstanding ingredients. One of the most sought-after lunch options is The Pig Club: a sandwich generously filled with slow-cooked leg of pork, chorizo, grain mustard, tomato and English leaf salad, and served with fries. Several interesting vegetarian dishes are also on offer.

The Pig on the Hill is at the heart of the community, with its games room, skittle alley and Pigstock festival – a celebration of local music usually held in May.

Specialities: The Pig Club, suckling pig, vegetarian mains

££

Daily from 11

Pusehill Road, Westward Ho!
EX39 5AH, 01237 459 222
www.pigonthehillwestwardho.co.uk

Getting There
Heading towards Barnstable on the A39, take the B3236 towards Westward Ho!. Turn left onto Cornborough Road, and left again onto Pusehill Road.

The Secret
The Pig on the Hill is named after a Vietnamese pot-bellied pig called Saigon who used to roam this very spot.

20

Rock Salt Café and Brasserie
Seven-course heaven

£ £

Sun–Fri 10–9.30,
Sat 8–9.30

31 Stonehouse Street, Plymouth
PL1 3PE, 01752 225 522
www.rocksaltcafe.co.uk

Getting There
Take the A374 out of Plymouth, turn
left up the one-way side street next to
the Lidl supermarket, and Rock Salt is
at the top on the right-hand side.

The Secret
*Rock Salt keeps bagging all kinds of
awards, from a Taste of the West gold
award to two coveted AA rosettes.
What will be next for this rising star?*

It's unlikely you'd stumble upon Rock Salt by chance,
given its position off the main drag. But soon after it
opened in 2011, this neighbourhood brasserie was
absolutely buzzing thanks to the power of word of mouth.

The lunch menu features an outstanding beef burger
served with mature cheddar, while the more elaborate
evening menu features venison with braised ox cheek,
bone marrow and red cabbage. Those who fancy
skipping meat altogether have lots of options, from the
black bream with Jerusalem artichoke to the 'forest
fungi' cannelloni with blue cheese.

Finally, for gourmets – hungry ones, at that! – there's
a seven-course tasting menu available every night.
Be sure to book this – and Rock Salt's regular
Pan-Asian evenings – well in advance.

Specialities: burgers, seven-course tasting menu

SERVICE 5

HEALTHY FOOD 5

AMBIENCE 5

Rock Pool Café
A fab fry-up

G V & 🍴 📶 ⛱ ♨

This busy seafront café is famous locally for its fry-ups – real crowd-pleasers that come with eggs, bacon, sausages, mushrooms, baked beans, buttered toast, golden hash browns and even chips. Feel free to chop and change ingredients, depending on what you fancy.

Also a great place for lunch, the café offers baguettes, paninis, homemade soup and delicious muffins and cakes. Or, for something more substantial, opt for one of the classic hot meals, such as the ham, egg and chips or bangers and mash.

Rock Pool Café is a top choice with families and surfers on their way to and from the beach that dominates Westward Ho!. Incidentally, this is the only place in the UK with a name that includes an exclamation mark.

Specialities:: cooked breakfasts, paninis, homemade soups

£

Daily 9–5

2 Golf Links Road, Westward Ho!
EX39 1LH, 01237 477 763
www.facebook.com/
RockPoolCafeWestwardHo

Getting There
This café is next to the Co-Operative supermarket, opposite the car park, at Golf Links Road's western end.

The Secret
This humble little café lies just a few steps from a golden sandy beach that stretches for a jaw-dropping 3km.

4
SERVICE

3
HEALTHY FOOD

3
AMBIENCE

RHS Rosemoor
A perfect picnic

Being a Royal Horticultural Society (RHS) garden, Rosemoor may not exactly be a secret, but we had to include it in this guide because of the award-winning food served in its on-site restaurant.

Every day, there are three hot main courses to choose from; these always include a vegetarian and a gluten-free option. Sandwiches, jacket potatoes and masses of fresh produce from the gardens also feature heavily.

While carveries don't always have a great reputation, the one here on Sundays (midday–3) is very good, and usually includes Exmoor-reared beef as one of the two meat choices. The half-portions of hot meals (which are half the price, naturally) are ideal for smaller people.

Entrance to the restaurant is free all year, but please note there is a charge to access the gardens.

Specialities: Sunday roasts, homemade cakes

Apr–Sep daily 10–5.30,
Oct–Mar daily 10–4.30

££

RHS Garden Rosemoor, Great Torrington
EX38 8PH, 0845 265 8072
www.rhs.org.uk/gardens/rosemoor

Getting There
Head south out of Great Torrington on the A3124 towards Winkleigh, and the entrance to RHS Rosemoor will be on your right.

The Secret
Order a picnic from the restaurant and go off into the gardens to enjoy the lovely selection of homemade treats outside. The jute picnic bags are reusable – an added bonus!

SERVICE

HEALTHY FOOD

AMBIENCE

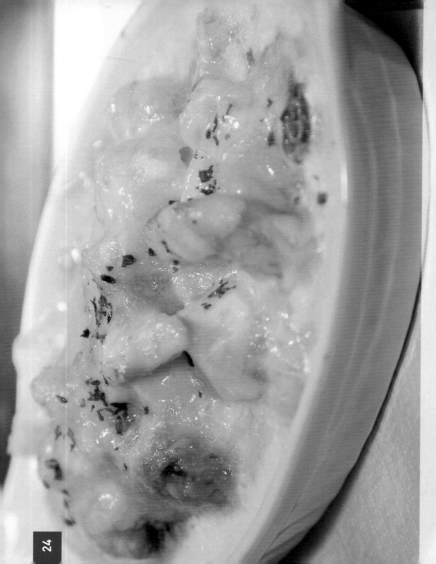

Fatbelly Fred's
Seafood sauciness

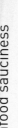 

SERVICE 4

HEALTHY FOOD 4

AMBIENCE 3

Tue–Sat 10–3 & 6–10

£££

16 Maiden Street, Barnstaple
EX31 1HA, 01271 345 700
www.fatbellyfreds.co.uk

Getting There
Fatbelly Fred's is on Maiden Street,
a pedestrianised lane right in the
centre of Barnstable.

The Secret
*This tiny restaurant was named after
the owner's baby son, who had a little
round belly after eating. Apparently, the
big belly now only applies to the owner,
and not necessarily after eating'.*

If you love seafood, you'll love Fatbelly Fred's. The
menu is one big celebration of the daily catch, with
dishes prepared by seasoned chefs who understand
the intricacies involved in cooking seafood to perfection.

All dishes can be tailored to your taste, so if you don't
fancy a particular sauce or side with your fish, you can
simply swap it for something else. The kitchen is more
than happy to oblige, which is ideal for pernickety eaters
or those with food intolerances.

And if seafood's not your thing, don't worry – there's
always a handful of alternatives, such as the delicious
pan-fried duck breast or the rich aubergine and courgette
bake. It's a good idea to put a call through before you
arrive, so you know what to expect that day.

Specialities: seafood platter, squid with aioli,
mussels Provençal

Terra Madre
The art of tapas

Broomhill, which is situated in the heart of the north Devon countryside, combines a hotel and restaurant with a sculpture garden. This beautifully designed open-air 'gallery', which dates from 1997, features a permanent collection of contemporary sculpture, including the striking *Big Red Shoe* by Greta Berlin, which sits at the hotel entrance.

Just as much of a joy as the art is the food served in Terra Madre, the award-winning on-site restaurant. Mediterranean slow food is the running theme here, with dishes made using organic ingredients from local farms. The three-dish tapas and homemade bread is delicious, while high tea (Wed–Fri 2.30–3.30) is a very civilised affair featuring homemade cakes and snacks. The restaurant is only open on certain days of the week, so booking is essential.

Specialities: tapas, charcuterie, high tea

Wed–Sun 12.30–1.30,
also Wed–Sat 7–8.30

££

Broomhill Art Hotel, Muddiford Road, Barnstaple EX31 4EX,
01271 850 262
www.broomhillart.co.uk

Getting There
Take the A39 north out of Barnstable, then turn left onto the B3230 towards Ilfracombe, following the signs after the North Devon District Hospital.

The Secret
Broomhill offers a range of gift ideas, including a three-course supper and overnight stay. See website for details.

5 SERVICE

5 HEALTHY FOOD

5 AMBIENCE

25

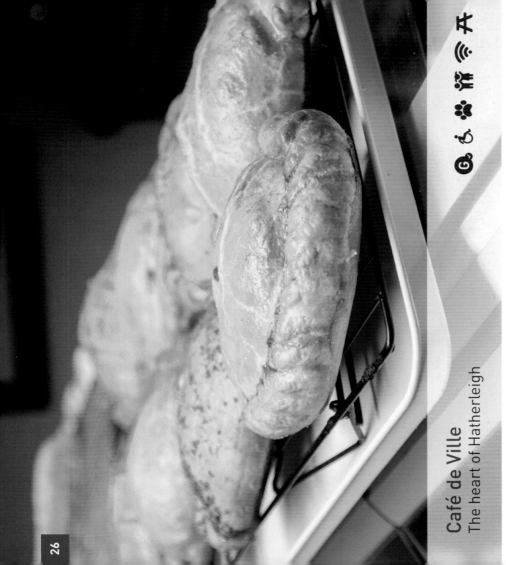

Café de Ville
The heart of Hatherleigh

£

Tue, Thu & Fri 9–5,
Wed & Sat 9–2.30

1 Market Street, Hatherleigh
EX20 3JN, 01837 810 582

Getting There
Café de Ville is just a 2-minute walk
from a large public car park in the
centre of Hatherleigh.

The Secret
*When you find a café with a deli
attached to it, you know the food
will be taken seriously – this place
is no exception. Be sure to stock up
on larder goodies on your way out.*

4 ⓘ SERVICE

3 HEALTHY FOOD

4 AMBIENCE

Café de Ville is a sweet café in the heart of the market
town of Hatherleigh. It's usually full of walkers and
cyclists in need of quick calories after a session on the
nearby Tarka Trail – a 290km track following the route
of Tarka the Otter in Henry Williamson's novel of the
same name.

The menu offers traditional café meals, from soup,
pasties, sandwiches and jacket potatoes to cakes
and cream teas. The breakfast menu includes porridge
and syrup, an all-day full English, and pretty well
everything in between.

If you get there early enough and the weather is
fine, grab a table in the lovely little courtyard
around the back. Dogs are welcome.

Specialities: pasties, homemade cakes, coffee.

Westward Café and Truckstop
A proper caff

♿ 🚐 👫

While you won't get a fine-dining experience at Westward Café and Truckstop, you're guaranteed some hearty English café food and the warmest of welcomes.

Dishes on offer here are of the stick-to-your-ribs variety, including homemade cottage pie, liver and bacon casserole and roast dinners. Portion sizes are generous and the café is clean, bright and reminiscent of one of the better greasy spoons of days gone by.

This is a great place to break a long journey to the West Country – it opens its doors very early in the morning and is much cheaper than your average service station. And no need to worry about parking because this is, first and foremost, a lorry drivers' café, so there's ample parking for cars and caravans.

Specialities: chip butties, full English breakfast

Lee Mill Bridge, Ivybridge PL21 9EE
01752 894 344

Mon–Thu 6–7.30,
Fri 6–2.30, Sat 8–2.30

£

Getting There
Turn off the A38 at Lee Mill and the Westward Café and Truckstop is attached to the Gulf petrol station on Plymouth Road.

The Secret
There's nothing particularly glamorous about this roadside café, but if you're after a decent fry-up on the road, you can't beat it.

5
SERVICE

3
HEALTHY FOOD

2
AMBIENCE

27

The Oyster Shack
Sensational shellfish

🛌		SERVICE	5
🌿		HEALTHY FOOD	5
		AMBIENCE	5

Daily midday–9

£££

Milburn Orchard Farm, Bigbury
TQ7 4BE, 01548 810 876
www.oystershack.co.uk

Getting There
The restaurant is on Stakes Hill, just off the A379 on the way to Kingsbridge. This is a tidal road; at high tide, come via the hamlet of St Anns Chapel.

The Secret
If you want to learn how to shuck oysters and prepare fish, sign up for one of the day-long Shack Fishing Trips. See website for details.

Twenty-five years ago, The Oyster Shack was just that – a very basic shack where locally caught oysters were cleaned in tanks before going to market. Locals would pitch up outside with picnic blankets, crusty bread and a bottle or two of wine to enjoy a long alfresco lunch featuring some of the freshest oysters in the southwest.

In a way, not a lot has changed since then. Though it was turned into a restaurant a few years ago, the Shack's distinctive heart and soul remain very much intact. This is a place where friends gather on tables under bright orange sail to share simple but sensational shellfish.

While you're here, visit the fishmonger's counter, where you can buy the freshest fish and shellfish at market prices.

Specialities: crab soup, moules marinière, gravadlax

The Birdcage
Pizza paradise

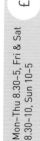

Mon–Thu 8.30–5, Fri & Sat 8.30–10, Sun 10–5

£

11 The Square, Chagford TQ13 8AA
01647 433 883
www.thebirdcagechagford.co.uk

Getting There
This café is easily found in Chagford's main square. There are a handful of parking spaces right outside, although they tend to fill up fast.

The Secret
The pizzas here are out of this world – just one reason The Birdcage has been awarded a much sought-after TripAdvisor Certificate of Excellence.

The Birdcage, on the main square in the Dartmoor town of Chagford, is something of a pilgrimage site for gourmet-pizza lovers. Available with gluten-free bases and in two sizes (9 and 12 inches), the pizzas come with a dozen or so different toppings to choose from.

The Rosso Bianco is particularly good, with rosemary-infused mascarpone sauce, mozzarella, juicy sun-blush tomatoes and sweet peppers. The kitchen is happy to swap toppings around, so don't be afraid to ask. If pizza's not your thing, the daily brunch, lunch and afternoon-tea menus have lots of variety and the Friday and Saturday tapas nights are superb.

If the weather's fine, sit at one of the outside tables under a sunshade. Otherwise, enjoy the richly coloured fabrics and quirky design details of the interior.

Specialities: pizzas, cakes, gluten-free dishes

5
SERVICE

4
HEALTHY FOOD

5
AMBIENCE

Mother Meldrum's Tea Gardens

Tea in the valley

The Valley of the Rocks is one of the most breathtaking beauty spots in the southwest. It's a big hit with walkers, photographers and other outdoor enthusiasts. Rather unusually, this steep basin runs parallel to the coast.

Mother Meldrum's Tea Gardens are tucked away at the bottom of the valley, surrounded by stunning scenery and watched over by the feral goats who roam the hills. It's a convenient spot for passers-by in need of a pick-me-up. Tuck into homemade pasties, sandwiches and all manner of sweet treats, including cream teas with huge scones and mincemeat and apple lattices. Also on offer are early-evening meals and a roast lunch on Sundays.

The large garden has plenty of picnic tables and is ideal for those with dogs. Inside, there's more seating, although take note: it can get very busy in the high season.

Specialities: cream teas, homemade pasties, cakes

The Valley of the Rocks, Lee Toad, Lynton EX35 6JH, 01598 753 667

Getting There

Take the road out of Lynton towards the Valley of the Rocks. As you head down the hill, Mother Meldrum's is hidden in a little piece of woodland on the right-hand side.

The Secret

Steeped in legend, this café is named after a folkloric witch who is said to have lived in the valley. Look out for the witch paraphernalia dotted around.

Mid-Mar-end Oct daily
10-5

££

SERVICE 5

HEALTHY FOOD 4

AMBIENCE 5

Harbour House Café
Deep breath... and relax

SERVICE 5

HEALTHY FOOD 5

AMBIENCE 4

£

Mon–Sat 10–5

Harbour House, The Promenade,
Kingsbridge TQ7 1JD
01548 855 666
www.harbourhousecafe.com

Getting There
Head down Fore Street and onto the
Promenade (A379). The café is on the left.

The Secret
*The sun-lit interior balcony is the best
place to sit at Harbour House Café
– it overlooks the local artworks in
the gallery below. In good weather,
the secluded garden is also lovely.*

The light and airy Harbour House Café is just a short
distance from the pretty estuary in the market town
of Kingsbridge. The town's only entirely vegetarian
establishment, the café uses fresh, seasonal, organic
and mainly allotment-grown ingredients in its dishes.

Light lunches here include healthy tagines and tarts,
paninis and pittas, soups and salads. The long list of
cakes that takes up half the menu is testament to the
owners' belief in the benefits of the occasional sugary
indulgence. And, as you'd expect, there's lots of choice
for vegans and those with food intolerances.

The café is part of the Harbour House Arts & Yoga
Centre, which also includes three yoga studios and an
art gallery, set in a lovely converted Georgian building.

Specialities: paninis, salads, cakes

Venue 72
Bringing home the bacon

SERVICE
④

HEALTHY FOOD
④

AMBIENCE
④

£££

Mon–Thu 7–7, Fri & Sat
7–11, Sun 9–5

72 South Street, South Molton
EX36 4AG, 01769 573 274
www.venue72.co.uk

Getting There
South Street is easy to access on
the B3226, one of the main streets
running through town. There's street
parking and a car park near by.

The Secret
*If you're too busy for a sit-down meal
at Bistro 72, either grab a takeaway
or – if you work in town – have your
meal delivered straight to your office.*

Apologies to all the other bacon-butty experts in North
Devon, but, according to Venue 72's regular customers,
the one on the menu here tops the list. Also legendary
are the full English breakfasts and the rather more
sophisticated eggs Benedict.

However, it's the seasonal bistro menu – available on
Friday and Saturday evenings – that really wins the
day at Venue 72. A typical dish might be pan-fried duck
breast served with a traditional Irish colcannon and
local, seasonal veg. Some dishes on the menu are
marked as 'slimming'; though they might be light on
calories, they're still as tasty as anything.

Eating at Venue 72, where you can bring your own
alcohol at weekends, is rather like dining with friends
– lively, relaxed and very good fun.

Specialities: bacon butties, full English breakfast

Fingle Bridge Inn
Old-fashioned pub grub

Perched on the banks of the River Teign, the Fingle Bridge Inn is in such a beautiful setting that you might be tempted to stay longer than planned. This traditional, family-run pub is close to several fairly easy walks along the river, which are ideal for families.

On the menu, you'll find good, old-fashioned pub grub, including classics such as ham, egg and chips, steak and ale pie and ploughman's lunches. For something a bit lighter, try a bar snack – delicious washed down with a locally brewed ale or cider – or a Devon cream tea (served midday–5). The renowned Sunday carvery gets very busy, so it's best to book ahead.

In winter, log fires warm the cosy interior, while balmy summer days are best spent on the riverside terrace.

Specialities: Sunday carvery, cream teas, ploughman's lunches

Daily midday–3 & 6–9

£

Drewsteignton EX6 6PW
01647 281 287
www.finglebridgeinn.co.uk

Getting There
From Exeter, take the A30 westbound. At Woodleigh junction, follow the signs to Crockernwell and then onwards to Fingle Bridge.

The Secret
The Fingle Bridge Inn has a large function room that can accommodate 120 people – ideal for weddings, parties, conferences and other events.

SERVICE
4

FOOD
HEALTHY
4

AMBIENCE
5

33

Pigs Nose Inn
In a world of its own

♿ 🚐 🏠 🐾 👫 📶 ⛲ ♨

£

5 SERVICE

3 HEALTHY FOOD

4 AMBIENCE

Daily midday–2 & 6.30/7–9 (closed Sun eve in winter)

East Prawle, Kingsbridge TQ7 2BY, 01548 511 209
www.pigsnoseinn.co.uk

Getting There
East Prawle is on the southernmost tip of Devon and the Pigs Nose Inn is in the centre of the village, opposite Piglet Stores, the village shop.

The Secret
The Pigs Nose Inn, which dates back 500 years, was once a smugglers' inn where booty from local shipwrecks was stored.

Entering the Pigs Nose, you feel like you've stepped into an alternative reality. Every corner, shelf and surface is bursting with knick-knacks and odd curiosities, from abandoned bits of knitting just waiting to be picked up and continued to sun-bleached animal skulls. Every artefact has a story – just ask at the bar if you'd like to know more.

The meals served at the Pigs Nose are the definition of basic, filling slap-up food – think chilli con carne, scampi and chips, and ploughman's lunches – and the hand-pumped beers are wonderful. Good news all round, when you consider the pub's proximity to the coast path and the many campsites that spring up in nearby fields in summer.

The pub is the beating heart of the village of East Prawle. It overlooks the pretty village green and the village shop – the equally eccentric Piglet Stores.

Specialities: paella, chilli con carne, fish and chips

Home Farm Café

Simplicity & style

The elegant country estate of Parke is situated on the edge of Bovey Tracey, with the wild expanse of Dartmoor beyond. Its acres of meadows, gardens and parkland are a great place to work up an appetite before heading to the on-site café for a lovely lazy lunch.

Home Farm Café is run by Stella West-Harling MBE, founder of the acclaimed Ashburton Cookery School, whose passion for genuine, earthy food is renowned.

Menu highlights include jacket potatoes with generous fillings and slow-cooked beef pasties. Evening meals, which are eaten by candlelight, put Dartmoor firmly in the spotlight, with locally raised beef, pork and lamb featuring heavily. Although not ideal for vegetarians, there's always a delicious meat-free dish on the menu.

Specialities: crispy Dartmoor pork belly, home-cured gravadlax, cream teas

Sun–Thu 10–5, Fri & Sat 10–5 & 7–late

£ to ££

Parke, Bovey Tracey TQ13 9JQ
01626 830 016
www.homefarmcafe.co.uk

Getting There
The National Trust-owned Parke estate is just 3km from the Devon Expressway (A38), which connects Plymouth and Exeter, about 2km outside Bovey Tracey.

The Secret
The Sunday-afternoon music sessions here work very well, allowing you to linger over a long lunch while listening to soulful numbers by local artists.

5 SERVICE

5 HEALTHY FOOD

5 AMBIENCE

Colourful crockery, Home Farm Café

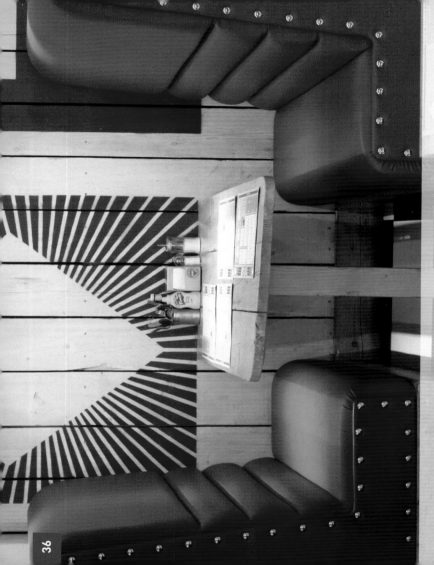

Ruby Modern Diner
Beef is the word

| £££ |

Daily 11.30–late

74 Queen Street, Exeter EX4 3RX
01392 436 168
www.rubyburgers.com

Getting There
From the city centre, walk along
Queen Street towards Exeter Central
station. The diner is on your right, by
the entrance to Northernhay Gardens.

The Secret
*If you can't decide which burger
to have, go for the sliders – three
half-size burgers of your choice
with two delicious side dishes.*

5 / SERVICE

4 / HEALTHY FOOD

5 / AMBIENCE

This 1950s-inspired diner offers an all-American
fast-food dining experience with a twist. All the meat,
cheese, beers and other ingredients served on site
are from West Country farms and producers. Even
the restaurant's name is inspired by a native breed of
cattle – the Red Ruby – which is supplied, in this case,
by nearby Copplestone Barton Farm.

There are more than a dozen different burgers on the
menu, as well as other exciting options, such as the
Notorious P.I.G. (pulled pork with slaw), the Turbo
Nachos (Ruby chilli with the works) and the veggie
'faloumi' burger (a falafel patty with halloumi).

A modern take on a traditional diner, this place is all
red leatherette booths and chrome mixed with rustic
wooden benches and tables.

Specialities: burgers, burgers and veggie burgers

36

The NoBody Inn
An epicurean's delight

This 17th-century inn has quite a reputation among epicureans, and rightly so. The menu is imaginative and extensive, and the bar bursts with 250 wines and 250 whiskies; the whiskies range from a nip at £2.35 to a whopping £95.90 a shot.

Typical dishes include pumpkin and sage risotto and confit fillet of sea bream with a soft herb crust, creamed leeks and potatoes. The cheese platter is a great alternative to pudding – simply tick your choices on the menu, hand it over and your platter will arrive. And if you're staying overnight, try the NoBody Night Cap – a selection of nine cheeses and half a bottle of port.

The low ceilings, blackened beams and inglenook fireplace in this pub create an atmospheric backdrop.

Specialities: cheese platter, steak and NoBody ale pie

££

Mon–Sat 11–11,
Sun midday–10.30

Doddiscombsleigh, Exeter EX6 7PS
01647 252 394
www.nobodyinn.co.uk

Getting There
Head into Doddiscombsleigh, situated between the A30 and the A38 to the southwest of Exeter, and the pub is in the heart of the village.

The Secret
If you happen to order the last shot of a rare whisky at this pub, the empty bottle is yours to take away.

5
SERVICE

4
HEALTHY FOOD

5
AMBIENCE

37

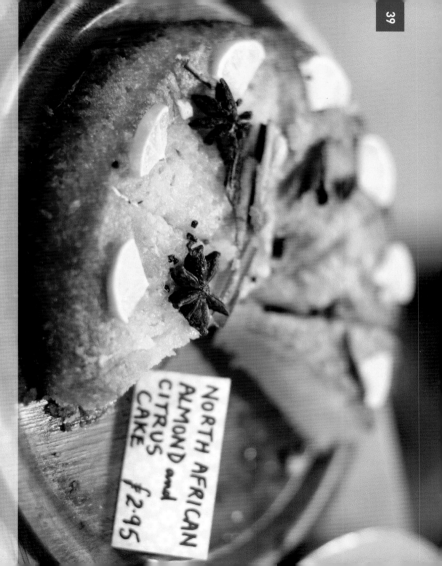

NORTH AFRICAN ALMOND and CITRUS CAKE £2·95

The Bakehouse

From teas to tapas

The Bakehouse is renowned for its Devon-roasted coffee, loose-leaf teas and homemade cakes. Savoury offerings include West Country-themed sharing platters and old café favourites with a modern edge. Try the Italian, a delicious toasted sandwich of salami, olives, mozzarella and tomato, and served with a pesto-mayonnaise dip. There are also soups, salads and jacket potatoes with a selection of fillings.

On Thursday, Friday and Saturday evenings, candles transform this bustling café into a sophisticated wine and tapas bar. At these times, sharing platters bursting with the flavours of Spain are typically washed down with a house cocktail or two. And, in case that wasn't enough, Wednesday nights are pizza nights, with twelve toppings to choose from.

Specialities: cakes, loose-leaf teas, tapas platters

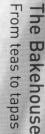

3 High Street, Cullompton EX15 1AB
01884 352 22
www.thebakehousecullompton.co.uk

Mon-Sat 9-5, also
Thu-Sat 6.30-11.30

££

Getting There

This café is easy to find on the high street. There is street parking outside and a couple of car parks nearby.

The Secret

A grocer's shop in Edwardian times, this building still has the original gold-leaf lettering on the outside and meat hooks on the inside. Old photos and original brickwork adorn the café interior.

SERVICE 5

HEALTHY FOOD 4

AMBIENCE 5

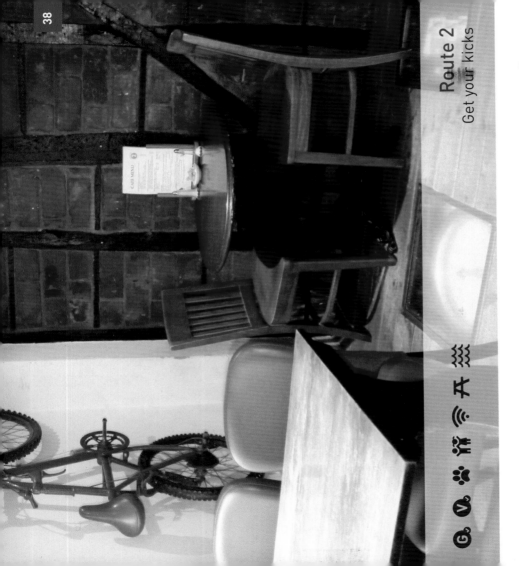

Route 2

Get your kicks

SERVICE 5

HEALTHY FOOD 5

AMBIENCE 4

£

Mon–Fri 8–5,
Sat & Sun 8–6

1 Monmouth Hill, Topsham Hill
EX3 0JQ, 01392 875 085
www.route2topsham.co.uk

Getting There
Route 2 is on the corner of the roundabout at the bottom of Fore Street. There is a large car park opposite, on the waterfront.

The Secret
In 2014, Route 2 was named by The Guardian as one of the top ten cycling cafés in the UK.

As its name suggests, this café is located on Route 2 – the National Cycle Network route which, when complete, will link Kent with Cornwall. A great stop-off point on the Exeter-to-Exmouth stretch of the route, this café has seating inside and out, room to keep your gear close by and bikes to hire from the adjacent shop.

The all-day breakfast includes sausages and bacon from the local butcher, while the Green Route is a veggie fry-up and the Half Route is a smaller plate. Route 2 prides itself on using the very best local produce, and almost everything is homemade, including the ice cream and 'real Dutch apple pie'.

In the on-site bar – which is the only one in Topsham – you can sample wines from the nearby Pebblebed Vineyard, as well as Devon beer, cider and juice.

Specialities: breakfasts, ice creams, local wines